Angel Alert!

Brian Ogden

Illustrated by Beccy Blake

Scripture Union

© Brian Ogden 2001
First published 2001

Scripture Union, 207–209 Queensway, Bletchley,
Milton Keynes, MK2 2EB, England.

ISBN 1 85999 494 6

British Library Cataloguing in Publication Data.
A catalogue record of this book is available from the
British Library.

Printed and bound in Great Britain by
Creative Print and Design (Wales), Ebbw Vale.

Contents

Chapter One

Donkeys don't make asses of themselves

The moment he sat on my back I knew there was something wrong. If you're a donkey you can tell these things. It's the way they wriggle about or tug the reins harder than usual. My master, Balaam, is usually quite kind. He makes sure I have enough to eat, and don't have to stand out in the hot sun all day. He remembers to make sure that I have plenty of water to drink.

Today was different. We set off on our journey with his two servants riding beside us. But Balaam was not in a good mood at all. Something must have made him cross. I found out later what was wrong – he was disobeying God. He was going to do something that God

had told him not to do.

What I knew, and what Balaam didn't know, was that an angel had arrived. The angel was standing in the middle of the road with a very sharp-looking sword in his hand. I didn't fancy an argument with a sword-swishing angel and trotted off the road into a field.

6

Balaam did something he never does –
he beat me with a stick.

I trotted back onto the road feeling
very unhappy with Balaam. Being
beaten for saving him from a sword-
swishing angel wasn't fair! We carried
on further down the road. On either
side of us, in the fields, were vineyards

with fine grapes growing on the vines. Guarding the vineyards were stone walls. The road narrowed between the walls.

By moving to one side I managed to squeeze past the angel. The only problem was that Balaam's foot was squashed against the wall. He was not a happy master! For the second time, he beat me with his stick. It really wasn't fair.

We carried on down the road. The further we went, the narrower it became. There was only just room for me to get past but standing in the way was… yes, you guessed! The angel! I couldn't squeeze past. I certainly couldn't jump over the wall with Balaam on my back! There was only one thing to do. I lay down in the road.

This time Balaam really lost his temper and started to beat me again. Then I had a surprise – and so did Balaam. I found I could talk to him.

Well, I've never had the chance to speak to Balaam before. I've always respected my master – gone where he wanted to go, carried what he wanted me to carry. I'm the only donkey he has ever had – we go back a long way together.

"Have I ever treated you like this before?" I asked.

"Well, er… no," Balaam replied.

Then God let Balaam see the angel. Well, you should have seen his face! There was the angel, sword and all, standing in the middle of the road. Balaam took one look and threw himself down in the road with his face on the ground. I've never seen him do that for anyone. It was quite frightening. There was Balaam and me on the floor with the angel standing over us with his sword.

The angel told my master that he had come to stop him from making this journey. The angel told Balaam that I, a donkey, had seen him and stopped three times.

By the time we got home we were friends. Balaam has never beaten me again – but then I've never seen another angel!

If you want to find out why the angel stopped Balaam, read the story in Numbers, chapter 22 and 23.

Chapter Two

No sheep, no cattle, no donkeys – no hope!

My name's Gideon. My family and I
have lived for the past seven years in
caves in the hills. Every moment of the
day we have to watch out for the
invaders. They have taken our sheep,
our cattle, our donkeys and our homes.
It all seems so hopeless.

Look down there –
they're thicker than
a swarm of locusts.

Life is very hard. We never know where our next meal is coming from. I had managed to grow a little wheat in a tiny field hidden from the view of the Midianites. I had cut the grain and was trying to thresh it in the old winepress. It was then I had a rather unexpected visitor. And it wasn't someone I knew.

I thought at first he might be one of those dreadful Midianite soldiers spying on us. But there was something different about him. I took a longer look and then I realised he was an angel. Angels are God's messengers. But the message he gave me was very strange.

I couldn't believe what he said.

"If the Lord is with us," I said to him, "then why have we got all these foreign soldiers in our country? It seems to me that the Lord has left us."

Then he said something even more unbelievable.

I started to make excuses. Not something you should do with an angel!

"But my family is the weakest of all of them," I said. "Not only that, but

I'm the least important member of my family. I am definitely not brave and mighty!"

I should have known better. I was never going to win the argument with this angel.

"You can do it because I will help you," said the angel. "You will crush the Midianites as if there was only one of them."

I wanted to laugh. Only one of them! There were *thousands* of them – remember what I said about locusts! There were so many Midianites down in the valley that it would take a year to count them! I needed some thinking time.

"Please don't go," I said, "until I bring you some food. If you really think I can drive out the Midianites then please give me some proof of who you are."

The angel sat down under the big oak tree that belonged to my father. He didn't seem in any hurry.

I ran back home thinking to myself what, if anything, do angels usually eat? I cooked some goat's meat. I remembered the wheat I had been threshing and ground the corn into flour and baked some fresh bread. It took some time but my visitor was still there when I took him the food. There was the meat, the bread, and the broth in which the meat had cooked. I hoped the angel would like it.

The angel was sitting patiently under the oak tree, holding a stick.

Well, you do what angels tell you, however strange it is. I put the goat's meat and bread on the rock. I poured out the broth like he said. It ran down over the meat, the bread and the rock. They were all soaked.

Then he did something quite amazing. He touched the meat and bread with his stick. The rock suddenly blazed with fire. The meat and bread were burnt although they were still soaking wet.

I turned away from the fire to speak to the angel – but he had gone! This was the proof. I had asked for proof and this was it. Only God could do these things. He really was an angel from God. And God really did want me to do great things for him.

My story doesn't end there. After lots of adventures, and with God's help, we did defeat the Midianites. We even drove them out of our land. But I never forgot the angel!

If you want to find out more about Gideon, read his story in Judges, chapters 6 to 8.

Chapter Three

Angel delight

Isn't it strange how a very good day can be followed by a very bad one? It was rather like that for me. By the way, my name is Elijah and I'm one of God's prophets. Prophets are people who pass on God's messages – sometimes to ordinary people and sometimes to kings.

My meeting with an angel happened when Ahab was king of Israel. Ahab was a very bad king – in fact he was just about the worst king the country had ever had. He did not worship God. He and his wife, Jezebel, worshipped Baal instead. Baal was the god that many people in the land believed would help them. Baal was not the true God.

One day, God gave me an important

message for King Ahab.

After I gave King Ahab the message, God told me to hide. That was good advice! Ahab looked everywhere for me. Two years went by and God told me to go back to the king. Then the most amazing things happened. You can read about them in the Bible but all I need to tell you now is that it did rain — very hard!

The king went home and told his wife, Queen Jezebel, what had happened. She was very angry because it was God who had made it rain. He had beaten the prophets of Baal; the god that Jezebel believed would help them. They couldn't even make it drizzle! Queen Jezebel sent me a message to say she was going to have me killed.

It was time to hide again. My good day had turned into a very bad one! I had had enough. I walked for miles into

the desert and wished I could die. At last
I fell asleep thinking I would never
wake up again. But it was then I had a
visitor.

The bread and water that the angel
brought tasted so good! Then I fell
asleep again. Once more, the angel
woke me with food and drink. This
time he told me I must go on a long
journey. I set off and travelled for forty
days until I reached Mount Sinai.

Mount Sinai is the holy mountain where God gave Moses the Ten Commandments. There, on the mountain, was a cave where I spent the night.

Caves are strange places. Sometimes if you shout loudly there is an echo.

It was God speaking to me. I tried to explain to him that I had always been his servant. I had always tried to do what he wanted. Now I was the only one left and Ahab and Jezebel wanted to kill me.

God told me to leave the cave and climb to the top of the mountain. As I climbed higher and higher the wind got stronger until it was blowing a gale. Rocks fell from the mountain and split as they hit the ground. Then I felt the whole mountain heave. It was an earthquake! I was terrified. After that the whole mountain seemed to be on fire.

The power of God was amazing but he didn't speak to me in the wind. He didn't speak in the earthquake or in the fire. After the fire went out I could just hear a soft whisper. I covered my face with my cloak and stood by the cave. I tried again to explain to God how I felt.

It was then that God told me what I was to do. I must hurry down to Damascus and appoint Elisha to be God's prophet after me. There was more good news – God promised that there would be seven thousand people in the land, not just me, who believed in him. God still had work for me to do.

You can read this story and more stories about Elijah in 1 Kings, chapters 17 to 19.

Chapter Four

An angel in the fire

My name is Daniel and I live in
Babylon. Babylon is not my home. I
was brought up in Jerusalem. When the
Babylonians attacked Jerusalem, the
soldiers took me, along with other
slaves, to Babylon. I try very hard to
pray to God and follow him even in a
foreign country.

There are four of us, all about the
same age, from Jerusalem. My friends
are Shadrach, Meshach and Abednego.
Nebuchadnezzar, the king of Babylon,
has treated us very kindly. He has made
sure that we have been well educated
and well fed. Now we all have
important jobs in Babylon. But there is a
big problem. The king has built a huge

statue – it's twenty-three metres high and three metres wide. Not only is it enormous, but it's also made of gold so you can't really miss it!

The Babylonians bowed down to the statue at once. Thousands of them all over the land worshipped it. But we do not believe in worshipping statues. We worship God in our prayers and by the way we live. There was a big problem when my friends wouldn't worship the statue.

The king flew into a right royal rage.
He ordered my three friends to be
brought to him. He asked them if it was
true that they had refused to worship
the statue. Then he gave them a second
chance. He warned them that if they
didn't bow down this time, they would
be thrown into the blazing furnace.

My friends were very brave. They
looked the king straight in the eye.

Nobody had ever seen the king so cross. His face was as red as the flames and his temper was blazing more fiercely than the furnace. He ordered his servants to heat the furnace seven times hotter than usual. He demanded that the strongest men in the army tie up my friends and throw them into the blazing inferno.

I was sure that I would never see my friends again. Still tied up they fell into the middle of the flames. I couldn't bear to look. Then the king, who had been sitting down to watch, suddenly leapt to his feet.

Everyone knew very well that only Shadrach, Meshach and Abednego had been thrown into the fire. There was no question of it – the officials agreed with the king.

King Nebuchadnezzar ordered
Shadrach, Meshach and Abednego to
come out of the furnace. By this time
word had got round the Court and
everyone, who was anyone, had come
to see my friends. And out they came,
completely unharmed. Their hair wasn't
singed, their clothes weren't burnt and
they didn't even smell of smoke! There
was nothing to show they had been
anywhere near the furnace.

The king was astonished by what had happened. Shadrach, Meshach and Abednego had disobeyed his orders and risked their lives rather than bow down and worship the statue. They had stayed true to the true God.

The result of their courage was that the king promoted them to better jobs. Shadrach, Meshach, Abednego and I never forgot that it was God's angel who saved them from the fire.

You can read this story in Daniel, chapter 3.

Chapter Five

Mary has a surprise visitor

As Mary told me later, it came as a very great surprise.

My name is Joseph. Mary and I are engaged to be married. One afternoon, Mary rushed into my little carpenter's shop in Nazareth looking very startled. I can remember exactly what I was doing when she arrived – mending old Benjamin's cart.

I sat Mary down on a broken chair I've never finished and she told me all about it.

Don't be afraid Mary, God has blessed you.

Whatever the angel said, I'm quite sure she was afraid: I would have been! He went on to tell her the most amazing things. God has chosen her to give birth to a son. This boy will be great and will be called the Son of the Most High God. He even told her what the boy is to be called – we are to name him Jesus. Poor Mary found it hard to understand everything the angel told her.

"How can this be?" she asked the angel.

The angel gave her the answer. He told her that God's power would rest upon her. Then the angel reminded her of the miracle that had happened with her cousin Elizabeth and her husband Zechariah. Despite both of them being very old, Elizabeth is going to have a baby. There is nothing, the angel reminded Mary, that God cannot do.

The angel left Mary and it was then that she came running over to tell me all about it. I couldn't believe it and told her so. Then that night I had a dream. In my dream an angel told me that what Mary had said was true. God has chosen my Mary to be the mother of his son, Jesus!

A few days later, Mary went off to visit her cousin Elizabeth. She stayed with Elizabeth and Zechariah in their home in the hills.

You are the most blessed of all women.

I missed her dreadfully but she had a good rest whilst she was there. She told me when she got home that a wonderful thing had happened when she met Elizabeth.

Elizabeth seemed to know all about Mary's baby and how he was going to grow into a very special person. Elizabeth and Mary shared their stories about the angel's visits and there was a lot of talk about babies! After three months, Mary came home again. A few weeks later, Elizabeth gave birth to John. When he grew up he became known as John the Baptist.

Several months after John was born, the soldiers came to Nazareth to tell everyone about the Roman census. We were ordered to travel from our home in Nazareth to the city of Bethlehem. It was there that Mary gave birth to Jesus in a stable behind an inn. It was there too that we heard about angels again.

Before Jesus was one day old, some very excited shepherds came bursting into the stable. They told us they had been looking after their sheep on the hillside above Bethlehem. Suddenly, a whole army of angels had appeared! The angels were singing praises to God.

And then, soon after the shepherds had gone, an angel came to me in a dream. There were many problems in the land and God sent him to us.

When it was safe to do so, we returned home to Nazareth where Jesus grew up. We often talked about the angels. Mary and I didn't see another one but I think Jesus met more angels when he was older.

You will find this story in Luke, chapters 1 and 2.

Chapter Six

The angel rolled
the stone away!

My name is Mary. My home is
Magdala, near Lake Galilee. For years I
was ill and nobody seemed able to make
me better – until I met Jesus. One
wonderful day he healed me and I
became a follower of his. Like so many
other friends I had gone with Jesus to
Jerusalem. Then what we most feared
had happened.

Last Friday, the saddest day of my
life, Jesus was put to death on a cross. It
happened because the leaders of the
Jews would not believe that Jesus really
was the Son of God. They wanted to
get rid of him. The only way to do that
was to make sure he died.

After Jesus died his body was taken

from the cross and buried in a tomb.
The tomb was rather like a small cave
dug out from the rock on the hillside. A
large round stone was rolled across the
entrance to the tomb so people couldn't
get in.

Saturday is the Sabbath, the day that
we keep holy. If I had visited the tomb
on the Sabbath I would have broken the
Jewish law. So I got up very early on
Sunday morning, before six o'clock, and
went out of the town and up the hillside
to where Jesus lay in the tomb. I wanted
to say goodbye to Jesus on my own but
when I got there I had a huge shock!

The great, round stone, that should have been guarding the tomb, had been rolled away. The entrance was open!

I ran back to the city of Jerusalem, through the early morning mist, to tell Peter and John. They were our leaders now Jesus had gone. I had to tell someone as soon as possible what I had found.

Peter and John ran off quickly leaving me to follow them. It seems that John got to the tomb first but didn't go in. Peter, when he arrived, went straight in and then John followed. What they saw was amazing.

The grave clothes that Jesus had been wearing were lying there but there was no sign of Jesus. It was then that Peter and John first believed that Jesus really had come back to life again.

By the time I got back to the tomb, Peter and John had gone. I was there on my own, desperately worried about Jesus. What had happened to his body? What could I do? I just stood there with the tears falling down my face. After a few minutes I found the courage to look into the tomb again. Imagine my surprise when I saw two angels! They were sitting where the body of Jesus must have lain in the cave.

The angels didn't answer me. They didn't need to. As I turned away from them, I realised that a man was standing close to me. At that moment I didn't know who he was. I only knew that he might be able to help me find Jesus. Just as the angels had done, he asked me why I was crying. I was sure, through my tears, that he must be a gardener working near the tomb.

If Friday had been the saddest day of my life, then Sunday was the happiest! As soon as I heard him call my name I

knew who it was at once. IT WAS
JESUS! He was alive again. The man
standing next to me was my friend and
master and he really was alive. I could
have stayed there for ever, I was so
happy. But Jesus had a job for me to do.

I think I ran even quicker than before
back to the city. This time I was
bursting to tell the others the wonderful
news. People who saw me running
through the streets must have thought I
was very strange. I was shouting,
"Alleluia!" and "Jesus is alive!" as I ran.

It was later that very day when Jesus came to see us. Most of his friends were together in a house in Jerusalem. He stood in the middle of the room and spoke to us.

Then Jesus did a wonderful thing. He showed us his hands and his side. We could see the scars from when he had been nailed to the cross. There was no doubt in anybody's mind: it was Jesus and he was alive! It made that Sunday happier still. It was the day the angels rolled the stone away.

You can read this story in John, chapter 20.

Chapter Seven

Inside out!

When an angel shakes you by the shoulder you wake up pretty quickly. Well, I certainly did! But let me explain how it all happened. My name is Peter and, at the time, I was in prison. I had been arrested on the orders of King Herod.

Soon after Jesus had returned to heaven, King Herod started to hunt down followers of Jesus. Some were killed because they believed in Jesus. Some, like me, were put in prison.

It was the middle of the night and very dark in my prison cell. I was chained to the guards, one on either side of me. There were more guards on duty at the prison gate. Herod was determined that I should not escape, but Herod had little idea of what God can do.

Fasten your belt and put on your sandals.

Somehow the angel had woken me without disturbing the guards. I rubbed my eyes and got dressed as quickly as I could. The angel led the way and I followed, still wondering if I was in a dream. We passed the first guard post and then the second. I tiptoed as quietly as possible past the soldiers but not one of them moved. Last of all was the great iron gate leading out of the prison into the city.

The gate just opened by itself to let us through and then we were in the street and out of the prison. It was then that the angel left me. It was also that I began to realise what had happened.

I stopped to think for a moment or two. It was still the middle of the night. I had to get off the streets in case the guards came searching when they found me missing. I needed to get to Mary's house. There would be many Christians in that house who were praying for me. They could take messages to the other leaders. I walked as quietly as possible through the streets until I reached the place, all the time making sure I wasn't being followed. I looked around but there was nobody about. It was safe to knock on the door. Rhoda, one of Mary's servant girls, came running to the door.

Rhoda was so happy to hear my voice that she ran back to the others without opening the door! All I could do was keep on knocking. The others didn't believe her but she insisted that she had heard me and at last they let me in.

They stood there singing and praising God that their prayers had been answered. After a time I held up my hand and managed to get some quiet. I told them how God had not forgotten me in prison. I told them about my amazing escape with the help of the angel, how not even the guards had woken up when my chains fell off, how even the great iron gate had opened for us.

Tell this to James and the rest of the believers.

It was time for me to move on. I had reassured my friends that I was all right but I couldn't leave them in danger. King Herod's men would know all about Mary's house. It would be the first place they would come to look for me in the morning.

I thanked my friends for their prayers and left whilst it was still dark. I knew of a safe place to hide in the city and went straight there.

There was a great uproar at the prison in the morning when the guards found out that I was missing. Not one of them knew how I had escaped. The king called his men together.

But God, who had sent an angel to rescue me, had other ideas. Search as hard as they could, the guards never found me. And that's the incredible story of how the angel took me from the inside to the outside!

You can find this story in Acts, chapter 12.

Chapter Eight

Shipwreck!

My name is Julius and I'm very proud to be a centurion in The Emperor's Regiment. As a Roman soldier I have had many duties over the years, but this one was different. My job was to take the prisoner, whose name was Paul, from Caesarea in Israel to Rome in Italy. This meant spending a long time at sea – not something I had ever enjoyed.

My men and a small number of prisoners, including Paul, set sail from Caesarea and the next day arrived in Sidon where Paul asked me a favour.

We set off again, passed the island of
Cyprus, and at Myra changed to a ship
that was sailing for Italy. Every day the
weather got worse. There were strong
winds and big waves. After a struggle,
we reached the island of Crete and
moored in the place called Safe
Harbours. There we stayed until the
captain of the ship convinced me it was
safe to move on.

Despite Paul's warnings, we left Safe Harbours and headed towards Phoenix, another port on Crete, and a better place for spending the winter. Soon after that our problems really started. At first, the gentle southern wind took us briefly along the coast but very soon a real north-easterly wind blew.

We had little idea of where we were being blown. It was getting more terrifying by the hour. The storm continued for days. We were soaked to the skin and frightened for our lives. On the Captain's orders the sailors threw the cargo and some of the ship's gear overboard to try to lighten the ship. We couldn't see the stars at night or the sun in the day. The waves kept crashing down on the deck. I was quite sure that the ship would sink and we would all drown. It was then Paul took over.

I thought he was mad. Nothing could save us from this awful storm but we had no other hope. Moments later we found that the sea was getting shallower by the minute. We must be near land. So much for Paul's angel! Now the ship was going to smash into rocks. That would be the end – nobody could live in that angry sea.

As the sun rose we saw we were just off the coast of an island. Not far away was a small bay with a sandy beach. It was then that Paul made his next suggestion.

I saw Paul take some bread. He gave thanks to God before he ate it. All of us ate some food and the Captain told me that he would try to run the ship onto the beach. As we headed towards what we thought was safety, the ship hit a

sandbank and stuck solid. The waves
continued battering the back of the ship
and it was being broken to pieces.

And that was how we got to the
shore. I counted the prisoners, the
soldiers and the crew. Despite the
storms, the rocks and the angry sea, no
one was missing. It was truly amazing!
Paul's angel had been right! We found
that we had come ashore on the island

of Malta. The islanders were very friendly and soon had a fire and some food ready for us.

Three months later we sailed away from Malta on a ship which had spent the winter on the island. At last, we reached Italy and I handed Paul over to other soldiers. It was a journey that I never forgot. I never forgot Paul either – he was an amazing man who believed in an amazing God. It was, after all, Paul's God who sent the angel which gave us the hope to carry on. And, I think, it was Paul's God who saved us.

You will find this story in Acts, chapter 27.